Contemplating
GOD
the Son

A Devotional

LAWRENCE KIMBROUGH

B&H
BROADMAN
& HOLMAN
PUBLISHERS

NASHVILLE, TENNESSEE

Ten-digit ISBN: 0-8054-4084-4
Thirteen-digit ISBN: 978-0-8054-4084-3

Published by Broadman & Holman Publishers
Nashville, Tennessee

Dewey Decimal Classification: 231.2
Subject Heading: GOD \ JESUS CHRIST \
DEVOTIONAL LITERATURE

Unless otherwise noted all Scripture is taken from
the Holman Christian Standard Bible® Copyright ©
1999, 2000, 2002, 2003 by Holman Bible Publishers.
Used by permission. Other versions include: NIV, New
International Version, copyright © 1973, 1978, 1984,
by International Bible Society; NASB, New American
Standard Bible, © the Lockman Foundation, 1960,
1962, 1963, 1968, 1971, 1972, 1973, 1975, 1977; used by
permission, and KJV, Kings James Version.

1 2 3 4 5 6 7 8 9 10   10 09 08 07 06

CONTENTS

INTRODUCTION

As long as you don't mind not knowing it all when you've finished, the Trinity can be a fun topic to lose yourself in for awhile. The relationship alone between the Father and Son—both equally God yet revealed to us in a manner that indicates dependence and double-sided affection—is enough to leave you awash in wonder.

For many of the slow-moving centuries after the death and resurrection of Christ, the debate over who Jesus was (and is) raged on in the gathered assemblies of holy thinkers and church officials. Yet even as late as our advanced age, where knowledge can whiz-bang in seconds between Boston and Beijing, this Three-in-One mystery can still only barely be explained using insufficient analogies about eggs and ice.

Thankfully, however, our walk with the Son of God isn't confined to head trips. Even in not telling us everything, he has told us all we need to know. That's why getting to think about him in the context of these devotional moments is sort of a bonus. Added value. Gravy. Were we never to know anything else about him, we would still know (at the least) that he has sacrificed himself for our sins and paved our pathway to paradise.

The rest is pure enjoyment.

What to Expect

Although I'm sure you'll find your own way to make this book work best for you, I thought I'd give you just a few ideas.

Most days don't lend themselves to a lot of quiet time with God. But then again, there are *some* days—perhaps early Sunday mornings, or a quiet afternoon, or the night before your day off—when you could really invest some extra time into worship, prayer, and Bible reading.

I'm thinking this collection of expanded devotionals would be perfect for that, especially because they include a whole bunch of related Scriptures to look up. That'll give God's Word a lot of opportunity to soak in.

Or perhaps you're the leader of some kind of Bible study—perhaps a men's prayer group or a handful of families who get together at someone's house once a week or so. This book ought to be a nice fit for you, then, because it keeps you on theme for a fairly long period of time and doesn't leave you short on material after five minutes. It's not too much, not too little. Maybe it will be just right for you.

But again, *you're* the one who knows best what you need. You're the one God has intrigued with the idea of discovering more about who he is. You're the one who's been thinking (rightly so) that spending some deliberate time with the Son will help make you more like him.

Me too. So let's get going. It ought to be fun.

ONE
THAT'S MY BOY

Try as we might, we parents will always be susceptible to the random temper flare-up, the occasional disappointed sigh, the vacant stare of inattention. We may genuinely enjoy watching our children practice ball, or make craft-stick log cabins on the kitchen table, or perform in the marching band. But there are some days when we tire at what this costs us—the time, the money, the videotaped episodes of our favorite show we'll probably never get around to watching.

We wear out. We wear thin. We don't always make sure to say, "I'm proud of you." "You did that really well." "I'm so glad the Lord blessed me with you."

But the Son of God has never known a day when he questioned whether or not his Father approved of him. He's never felt small, unimportant, or in the way. He's never gotten the impression that this probably isn't a good time to talk.

Look at Jesus' confidence as you read the Gospels. Get a sense of the comfort he feels with who he is. Notice his total peace about things, his calming presence. These are the clear marks of someone who's assured of his Father's love.

Father, help me to realize that because of your Son, I am fully approved of in your eyes, just as he is.

Jesus replied, "I assure you: The Son is not able to do anything on His own, but only what He sees the Father doing. For whatever the Father does, the Son also does these things in the same way. For *the Father loves the Son and shows Him everything He is doing,* and He will show Him greater works than these so that you will be amazed. And just as the Father raises the dead and gives them life, so the Son also gives life to anyone He wants to. *The Father,* in fact, judges no one but *has given all judgment to the Son,* so that all people will honor the Son just as they honor the Father. Anyone who does not honor the Son does not honor the Father who sent Him. . . .

"If I testify about Myself, My testimony is not valid. *There is Another who testifies about Me,* and I know that the testimony He gives about Me is valid. You have sent [messengers] to John, and he has testified to the truth. . . .

"But I have a greater testimony than John's because of the works than the Father has given Me to accomplish."

You can certainly imagine a scenario where Christ could have come to Earth, done what he did, and returned to heaven sinless and successful without needing any more than his Father's enabling, his Father's equipping, his Father's all-wise will and perspective.

But this wasn't merely a business transaction they were conducting, the logical tracings of some schematic diagram. Christ's ministry was never intended to be a matter-of-fact, fill-in-the-blank fulfillment of biblical prophecy.

Jesus hadn't come here with just his Father's *plan* but with his Father's *love.*

Stack that truth up against the other religions of the world, and see if anyone can't tell the difference. Feast your eyes on a Father who considered his approval and blessing every bit as vital to the Son as his power and might.

That's why the Father chose to send the Son to earth with much more than an expense account and a tool belt. When Jesus went to bed each night, he didn't pull out the blueprints he had brought with him from home, double-checking to be sure he'd remembered everything, that he was still on schedule and under budget.

He simply wrapped himself in the blanket of his Father's love.

READ
JOHN 3:34–35

Whether he closed his eyes in prayer or in peaceful sleep, Jesus could sense his Father's affection, not just his direction.

THE FAMILY TRUST

Love, though, is a hard word to define. We undoubtedly love our children, knowing full well that it's more than just the way we feel about them. We share a unique relationship. We get pleasure from their smile, their laugh, their familiar tone of voice. We hurt when life overwhelms them, and we burst with pride when they taste new hopes and heights of achievement.

Yet a big part of love (we learn as they grow) means putting *trust* in our children, giving them our nod of approval, letting them see for themselves what they can do.

Jesus, of course, was never in danger of taking on a responsibility that was too big for him. Training wheels or no, he was always assured of steering a straight line. He was "God with us," emphasis on the "God." Still, this doesn't take away from the fact that he needed to know he had his Father's full backing and support.

"By what authority are You doing these things?" the Pharisees were fond of asking (MATT. 21:23). "Who is it who gave You this authority?" (LUKE 20:2). The answer is: he *came* here with it. He showed up the first day with the authority from on high to forgive sins, to drive out demons, even to lay down his very life and take it up again. "I have received this command from My Father," he said (JOHN 10:18) . . . and had been trusted to use his power well.

READ
MATTHEW 28:18–20

5

More Than Acceptable

You can take a lot of comfort knowing that "in the future, you will see the Son of Man seated at the right hand of the Power and coming on the clouds of heaven" (MATT. 26:64). You can feel a bounce of relief in your aching heart, confident in the hope that one day "you will see heaven opened and the angels of God ascending and descending on the Son of Man" (JOHN 1:51).

This will be the ultimate display of the Son's acceptance and approval, when you see him glorified and highly exalted, when you hear him given "the name that is above every name" so that every tongue can confess that "Jesus Christ is Lord, to the glory of God the Father" (PHIL. 2:9, 11).

But believe it or not, you and I have been marvelously included in this family reception. When we received the grace of Christ by believing on his name, we also received the gift of the Father's full love and acceptance, delivered to us "through the one man, Jesus Christ" (ROM. 5:17).

Therefore, when that voice announced from heaven, "This is My beloved Son. I take delight in Him" (MATT. 3:17), the Father could see our face in his, our sins upon his hands and shoulders, our life in his resurrected body.

Marvel again at the wonder. God has blessed us beyond measure through the Son.

READ
EPHESIANS 1:3–6

DIG IN

John 5 says that when it comes to the relationship between the Father and the Son, you can't know one without the other.

"THE FATHER LOVES THE SON AND SHOWS HIM EVERYTHING HE IS DOING" (v. 20). Is this a capability that extends to believers as well—the knack for knowing where God is working?

....
....
....
....
....

"THE FATHER . . . HAS GIVEN ALL JUDGMENT TO THE SON" (v. 22). Why would the Father think it necessary to tell us that he had handed off this assignment—or any assignment—to the Son?

....
....
....
....
....

"THERE IS ANOTHER WHO TESTIFIES ABOUT ME" (v. 32). This kept Jesus from being dependent on his opinion polls. How could it help to cut down on your own mood swings?

....
....
....
....
....

Experiencing God the Son Over and Over Again

1. THE SON HAS THE FATHER'S BLESSING AND APPROVAL.
   Even though the Son of God needed nothing else in order to be totally complete within himself, the Father still chose to surround him with his love and support. It's an important reminder of the impact our approval as parents has on our children, as well as the impact the Father's approval through Christ should have on us.

2. THE SON SEEKS AND CARRIES OUT THE FATHER'S WILL.

3. THE SON REVEALS THE FATHER'S IDENTITY TO US.

4. THE SON IS THE FULFILLMENT OF LAW AND PROPHECY.

5. THE SON CAME HERE TO SERVE, TO GIVE, TO DIE.

6. THE SON SEEKS AFTER AND SAVES THE LOST.

7. THE SON IS THE MEANS OF OUR SALVATION.

8. THE SON REWARDS HIS PEOPLE WITH ETERNAL LIFE.

9. THE SON MEDIATES BETWEEN US AND THE FATHER.

10. THE SON IS THE FOUNDER OF THE CHURCH.

11. THE SON IS THE GIVER OF TRUE UNITY AND PEACE.

12. THE SON ENABLES OBEDIENCE IN HIS DISCIPLES.

13. THE SON DEMANDS OUR FULL TRUST AND LOYALTY.

14. THE SON IS COMING AGAIN.

PRAY ABOUT

- Any unmet approval needs that cloud your relationships.
- The freedom of living today in the Father's love and blessing.
- Your own desire to be more like Christ in every aspect of life.

TWO

YOURS AT COST

More than once, especially through those late teen years when I was seeking God's wisdom particularly hard in the area of college choices and job options, I remember picking up a few of those "how to know God's will" books, anxious to see if I could zero in on his direction for my life.

I'm not sure exactly what I was hoping to find in there. Certainly I wasn't fool enough to think I'd come across some kind of compass reading that would steer me by radio frequency into the future. No matter what the authors promised, I knew I was in for some hard work. A lot of listening. A lot of praying. A lot of watching for spiritual signals.

I wonder: *what would the Son of God know about how it feels to be long on questions and short on answers?* He was in the unique position of knowing full well what his future held. Yet even in being totally informed about the Father's plan for his life, he allowed himself to experience the same thing required of us in discerning God's path.

He had to seek it, and want it, and, if necessary, make unthinkable sacrifices to obtain it.

Lord Jesus, to see you obediently, passionately seeking the Father's will makes me wonder why I do it so halfheartedly. Change me. Make me want him.

When they found Him on the other side of the sea, they said to Him, "Rabbi, when did You get here?"

Jesus answered, "I assure you: You are looking for Me, not because you saw the signs, but because you ate the loaves and were filled. Don't work for the food that perishes but for *the food that lasts for eternal life, which the Son of Man will give you,* because God the Father has set His seal of approval on Him."

"What can we do to perform the works of God?" they asked.

Jesus replied, *"This is the work of God: that you believe in the One He has sent. . . .*

"But as I told you, you've seen Me, and yet you do not believe. Everyone the Father gives Me will come to Me, and the one who comes to Me I will never cast out. For I have come down from heaven, *not to do My will, but the will of Him who sent Me.* This is the will of Him who sent Me: that I should lose none of those He has given Me but should raise them up on the last day. For this is the will of My Father: that everyone who sees the Son and believes in Him may have eternal life."

I wonder how much of God's will we miss because we're too busy wanting chicken wings.

That was pretty much the disciples' problem in John 4. After looking up from a hard morning of baptizing, with a full sun bringing that noontime rumble into their stomachs, they figured they'd earned their break. Whatever God expected of them for the rest of the day, surely it could wait until after 1:00. Because somewhere within nose range, meat was in the oven. Bread was baking. It was lunchtime. And they had no intention of missing out.

I'm sure Jesus was hungry too. Even the Son of God knew how to enjoy his fish and his grains and all the other good food groups. But there was a slot at the top of his food pyramid that doesn't show up on the one they print on the back of our cereal boxes, a serving sample that makes up for its lack of calories by leaving behind the most pleasant aftertaste known to man.

That's why, when the disciples returned from town, spreading out their napkins and passing out their portions, they found that Jesus had already eaten. *Aw, come on and join us anyway!* they said.

No, thanks. "I have food to eat that you don't know about" (JOHN 4:32) . . . like giving new life to a five-timing Samaritan woman by the side of Jacob's well, the same watering hole the disciples had only seen as a way to wash down their sandwiches.

> READ
> JOB 23:11–12

WANT TO?

So is this why the will of God remains such a mystery to most of us? Would it stay less cloudy in our minds if we were just hungry enough for it? Are his purposes always sure to be lost on those who favor the soup of the day over the bread of life?

Would we know God's will if we really wanted to?

As simplistic as it may sound, I think the answer is yes. "If anyone wants to do His will, he will understand whether the teaching is from God or if I am speaking on My own" (JOHN 7:17). That was Jesus' response to those who were less interested in being changed than they were in being right, who weren't looking for reasons to enter in but for excuses to stay out.

Apparently there's something in calling him "Lord, Lord" that's supposed to equate to knowing—and doing—the "will of [our] Father in heaven" (MATT. 7:21). Not knowing what he wants us to do is most likely an indication that we don't want to do it.

I'm not saying that this necessarily means we can know with absolute assurance that we're supposed to make a certain career move, or attend a certain church, or choose a certain piano teacher for our children. But we can know that our heart's desire to follow God should result in obedience to the things we do know.

And our obedience to the things we do know—his revealed will, made plain in the Scriptures—will result in our walking faithfully into the unknown.

READ
2 CORINTHIANS
8:8–12

FIXED COSTS

After all, which is harder—walking into an unfamiliar tomorrow, unsure of what dangers it holds or walking into a future that you already know is filled with trial and torture?

I mean, we marvel that Jesus was able to endure the cross. And that's just by trying to relate to the physical aspect of it. We have no reference point to sense the infinitely more cruel spiritual punishment he underwent. Oh, sure, we know what our own guilt feels like, spread out over a lifetime of experiences. Imagine multiplying that weight millions of times, then compressing it into the tail end of a single week.

So when the Son cried out to the Father, "If You are willing, take this cup away from Me—nevertheless, not My will, but Yours, be done" (LUKE 22:42), he was declaring a level of surrender deeper than anything we could ever duplicate.

Yet in our own way, in our own decisions about what we'll accept in order to comply with God's will, we must realize this: either we'll want it at all costs, or we'll live with the stubbornly high taxes of our own self-preservation.

READ
ACTS 21:10–14

DIG IN

See Jesus looking strong and authentic in John 6, especially when seen side by side with human nature at its most pitifully petty.

"THE FOOD THAT LASTS FOR ETERNAL LIFE, WHICH THE SON OF MAN WILL GIVE YOU" (V. 27). What can we do to make eternity become a compelling motivator in our lives?

....
....
....
....

"THIS IS THE WORK OF GOD: THAT YOU BELIEVE IN THE ONE HE HAS SENT" (V. 29). We would expect our "work" for God to be defined by a more active verb than "believe." Why isn't it?

....
....
....
....
....

"NOT TO DO MY WILL, BUT THE WILL OF HIM WHO SENT ME" (V. 38). What's keeping you from saying these words, believing these words, living these words?

....
....
....
....

Experiencing God the Son Over and Over Again

1. The Son has the Father's blessing and approval.
2. The Son seeks and carries out the Father's will. So here's the prayer of the Son to his Father: "Your kingdom come. Your will be done on earth as it is in heaven" (Matt. 6:10). And for those of us who learn day by day to desire this more than anything, we get to share the experience: the blessing of living out our calling as his brother, his sister, his family in the faith (Matt. 12:50). No plans of ours could ever top that.
3. The Son reveals the Father's identity to us.
4. The Son is the fulfillment of law and prophecy.
5. The Son came here to serve, to give, to die.
6. The Son seeks after and saves the lost.
7. The Son is the means of our salvation.
8. The Son rewards his people with eternal life.
9. The Son mediates between us and the Father.
10. The Son is the founder of the church.
11. The Son is the giver of true unity and peace.
12. The Son enables obedience in his disciples.
13. The Son demands our full trust and loyalty.
14. The Son is coming again.

Pray About

- Getting a renewed awe for the Son's humility and submission.
- Surrendering whatever it is that stands between you and him.
- Doing his will today and worrying about tomorrow, tomorrow.

THREE

INSIDE
INFORMATION

I f God ever chose to give us a Moses moment, if he somehow passed before our eyes where we could even get a quick glimpse from behind (EXOD. 33:18–23), we'd never stop talking about it.

People would hear about us. They'd ask us to come speak in their churches, advertising our name on the block-letter billboard out front and with inserts in the bulletin. We'd be a show-and-tell surprise hit at our kids' school, maybe even a one-night wonder on *Larry King Live.*

Seeing God and living to tell about it—all five or ten seconds of it—would be the defining event of our lives.

But when the Son of God came to earth, he arrived with an eternity full of firsthand stories and information about the Father. He could gaze out across the gravel-crunching, dust-swirling, slowly dying landscape of human experience, realizing that the secrets he carried inside him held the promise of new life.

Imagine knowing what he knew, having seen what he'd seen. Don't you know he lived to tell the world about his Father?

Lord Jesus, if you hadn't told us about the Father, we'd never have known him. My prayer today is that you will make him known through me.

"In My Father's house are many dwelling places; *if not, I would have told you.* I am going away to prepare a place for you. If I go away and prepare a place for you, I will come back and receive you to Myself, so that where I am you may be also. You know the way to the place where I am going."

"Lord," Thomas said, "we don't know where You're going. How can we know the way?"

Jesus told him, "I am the way, the truth, and the life. No one comes to the Father except through Me.

"If you know Me, you will also know My Father. From now on you do know Him and you have seen Him."

"Lord," said Philip, "show us the Father, and that's enough for us."

Jesus said to him, "Have I been among you all this time without your knowing Me, Philip? *The one who has seen Me has seen the Father.* How can you say, 'Show us the Father'? Don't you believe that I am in the Father and the Father is in Me? The words I speak to you I do not speak on My own. *The Father who lives in Me does His works.* Believe Me that I am in the Father and the Father is in Me. Otherwise, believe because of the works themselves."

We take a lot of comfort in knowing that Jesus was "tested in every way as we are" (Heb. 4:15). But what ought to amaze us more, really, is that he was tested in ways we'll never be . . . and still maintained his straight-path walk of purity.

Try to picture, for example, what went on in his mind every time some showboat Scripture reader glared back at him with that thick, double-chinned condescension . . . as if this Nazarene hammer-slinger actually thought he understood God better than *he* did. What violent, tempting thoughts must have flared across the back wall of Jesus' imagination. What steely restraint it must have taken to stare into eyeballs and facial features he had fashioned in his own creative mind, now glazed over with proud contempt and pious disrespect.

Oh, sure, Jesus responded in strength. He didn't just smile silently in return while handing them a daisy. He continued boldly to reveal the Father's name and character to everyone he was led into contact with.

But my, what he could have done. My, what those people didn't know. My, how brave and daring it was for the Son to tell a skeptical world that the Father was here in the flesh and that Jesus himself offered the only way to know him.

READ
JOHN 10:31–39

THROUGH THE LOOKING GLASS

Truly among the great mysteries of God is the fact that "no one knows the Son except the Father, and no one knows the Father except the Son" (MATT. 11:27). And it would have stayed like this forever if the Father had not chosen through his own grace and mercy to make himself known also to "anyone to whom the Son desires to reveal Him" (V. 27).

Inside of this incredible truth are doctrines that strike our human ears like broom handles and trash can lids. For instance, after telling his parable of the sower—the one about the seed and the four types of soil—Jesus said to his followers that these "secrets of the kingdom of heaven have been given for you to know, but it has not been given to them" (MATT. 13:11).

Why not? we wonder. *That's not fair! Those people have just as much right to this revealed truth as anybody!* Yes, they do. Yet speaking with a wisdom known only to the living God, Jesus opened for us the hearts of the unredeemed when he said: "Looking they do not see, and hearing they do not listen or understand" (v. 13). It's not that their fate has been coldly determined. It's that their condemnation has been justly deserved.

READ
1 JOHN 5:19–20

The only thing we know for sure about why some are saved and some are lost is that if the Son hadn't told us what he knew, none of us would ever have known the Father at all.

SHOW ME

But he didn't just tell us. He showed us.

The Father's nature and essence is such that it can't merely be described or defined or diagrammed in a sentence. His justice and authority, his peace and long-suffering must be *demonstrated* in order even to come close to being captured.

This accounts for the genius in the Father's sending the Son with arms, legs, and real, human tears. This accounts for the blind eyes being fired with renewed color and motion, the slumped backs straightened again into youthful grace and stature, the dead and buried put back on the pink soles of their feet.

As Jesus said to his disciples in John 14, he had already given them enough of the Father's words to draw them into belief. But if words weren't sufficient for them, "believe because of the works themselves" (v. 11). *Believe because I have left you no doubt that I and the Father are really one . . . and really real.*

READ
HEBREWS 1:1–3

Be cautious of ever letting Jesus become so human that he loses his Godness in your eyes. Because when we see him, we see the Father. And we are saved.

DIG IN

The oneness between Father and Son, and the love between the Son and his people, find near poetic expression in John 14.

"IF NOT, I WOULD HAVE TOLD YOU" (v. 2). This is honesty at its purest, trust at its most authentic. Why do we so often live as if he's holding out on us, or as if he's of questionable reliability?

....
....
....
....

"THE ONE WHO HAS SEEN ME HAS SEEN THE FATHER" (v. 9). What would you say, then, that you absolutely know (and are still learning) about the Father as a result of knowing his Son?

....
....
....
....
....

"THE FATHER WHO LIVES IN ME DOES HIS WORKS" (v. 10). Can we receive this statement as our own? Is it fair to say that the works we do are the works of God?

....
....
....
....
....

Experiencing God the Son
Over and Over Again

1. The Son has the Father's blessing and approval.
2. The Son seeks and carries out the Father's will.
3. The Son reveals the Father's identity to us.
   If the words and the works of the Son bear testimony to the character of the Father—and if the life of the Son has given us rebirth as God's children—then we, too, bear both the responsibility and privilege of letting our Lord be evident in our lives. In this we become like the Son, finding our greatest joy when the Father reaches our friends by reaching through us.
4. The Son is the fulfillment of law and prophecy.
5. The Son came here to serve, to give, to die.
6. The Son seeks after and saves the lost.
7. The Son is the means of our salvation.
8. The Son rewards his people with eternal life.
9. The Son mediates between us and the Father.
10. The Son is the founder of the church.
11. The Son is the giver of true unity and peace.
12. The Son enables obedience in his disciples.
13. The Son demands our full trust and loyalty.
14. The Son is coming again.

Pray About

- Being constantly aware whose name we bear and represent.
- Those whom God is drawing to himself through our example.
- Never forgetting the grace and goodness that led us to him.

FOUR
ALL TOGETHER NOW

Maybe it's because most of us own about five or six Bibles apiece. Maybe it's because our main one is just another item on an ordinary list of essentials (like car keys and a cell phone) that we grab before heading out the door on Sunday morning. Maybe it's because we're so accustomed to seeing it by our bedside, surrounded by things like tissue boxes, nail clippers, and empty water glasses.

It's just easy to forget what a wonder our Bible is.

And among its most incredible properties is the fact that it hangs together from start to finish, without ever contradicting itself or losing its place.

Think of it: you and I can hardly keep one thought in our heads for more than five minutes. But God constructed the Bible in such a way that it not only stayed consistently true over the many centuries it was written in, but it still remains impeccably true to this day.

That's why, when the Son of God came to Earth, his birth announcement had already been in the mail for thousands of years.

Lord Jesus, when we begin to worship you, it's no wonder we don't know where to stop. Your life extends forever in all directions. You truly amaze us!

We ourselves proclaim to you *the good news of the promise* that was made to our forefathers. God has fulfilled this to us their children by raising up Jesus, as it is written in the second Psalm: "You are My Son; today I have become Your Father."

Since He raised Him from the dead, never to return to decay, He has spoken in this way, "I will grant you the faithful covenant blessings made to David." Therefore He also says in another passage, "You will not allow Your Holy Spirit to see decay." For David, after serving his own generation in God's plan, fell asleep, was buried with his fathers, and decayed. But the One whom God raised up did not decay. Therefore, let it be known to you, brothers, that through this man forgiveness of sins is being proclaimed to you, and *everyone who believes in Him is justified from everything,* which you could not be justified from through the law of Moses. So beware that what is said in the prophets does not happen to you: "Look, you scoffers, marvel and vanish away, because *I am doing a work in your days,* a work that you will never believe, even if someone were to explain it to you."

Imagine emptying your pockets of loose change every day when you get home, and each time you do—*every single time* for an entire year—you pour out exactly the same combination of nickels, dimes, and quarters.

The folks who first started seeing the connection between Old Testament prophecy and the risen Messiah must have had that same uncanny feeling. The more they counted and recounted, the more they studied and surmised, they discovered they had totaled up more than three hundred prior references to Christ, each one having been made many generations before his appearing.

And all of them had come true.

From the details of his birth to his long-standing family line, from his hometown to his donkey ride into Jerusalem, from specific information about his death to the owner of his three-day tomb—it's all there. Scattered from Amos to Isaiah and all points on the biblical map, the story of Jesus carves a straight line from back to front, never curving to accommodate slight bobbles in calculation or to make historical adjustments based on updated info.

Some people find it hard to believe that the Son of God's appearance into human history was already planned and in the mind of the Father from the virgin edges of eternity.

But I'll tell you what: you've got to wonder how he kept that many people on message for that long.

> READ
> ROMANS 1:1—4

MISTER RIGHT

But this miracle is much more than a mathematical phenomenon, a magic run against incredible odds. The result of this point-by-point, promise-keeping precision is that Christ has fulfilled every expectation placed on him by the law—a level of flawless obedience we fouled up before we even struggled our newborn bodies into the light of day.

"For if a law had been given that was able to give life, then righteousness would certainly be by the law" (GAL. 3:21). But the only way we were going to get within a galaxy of God's approval was for someone to go before us—a man who could perfectly obey the law from the inside out. "For just as through one man's disobedience the many were made sinners, so also through the one man's obedience the many will be made righteous" (ROM. 5:19).

That's where this doctrine gets personal. That's where theology books quit reading like a lecture and look more like a lifesaving device. The Son's pure fulfillment of law and prophecy is what

> READ
> MATTHEW 5:17—20

places us in the eternal flow of God's saving grace.

And for this we owe him everything.

Still Going Strong

Bottom line, the Son has gone to a great deal more trouble for us than we realize. (Yes, *trouble* definitely understates the lengths of his love. But then, what word doesn't?) It's more than the blood and agony, as horrific as these were. It's more than the steady resistance of temptation, as heroic as this was to accomplish. It's more than the heaped-up abuse and intolerance, as hard as these must have been to bear.

Jesus refused to let one promise fall to the ground half full. He knew in advance and fulfilled in time all the prophecies made about him, every hope of every Spirit-filled seer who, like Simeon, looked forward to Israel's consolation being satisfied in the coming of God's Messiah (LUKE 1:25–27).

What room do we have for doubt, then, that the Son is *still* fulfilling prophecy, *still* honoring Scripture, *still* awaiting the Father's summons to come and rescue us, to take us away with him forever into a place of sinlessness, safety, and sanctuary?

If he has been true this long, why not a while longer? Why not this afternoon, when your need for his help may be more raw and unvarnished than usual? Why not this week, when weighty decisions are keeping you up nights and inordinately occupying your conversations?

Why not you? Why not now? Why not just believe he is who he has always been?

READ
ROMANS 3:21–26

DIG IN

Of all the "new and improved" and "better than ever" promises we've heard, none can top the wonder of Acts 13.

"THE GOOD NEWS OF THE PROMISE" (V. 32). Try coming up with as many other "good" adjectives as you can think of to describe what the long-lasting promises of God are like.

....
....
....
....

"EVERYONE WHO BELIEVES IN HIM IS JUSTIFIED FROM EVERYTHING" (V. 39). Of all the ways our flesh can abuse this faith-based freedom, what are some ways our spirits can grow in it?

....
....
....
....
....

"I AM DOING A WORK IN YOUR DAYS" (V. 41). Some people are still living and praying and acting like God closed up shop two thousand years ago. How do you know that's not true?

....
....
....
....
....

Experiencing God the Son Over and Over Again

1. The Son has the Father's blessing and approval.
2. The Son seeks and carries out the Father's will.
3. The Son reveals the Father's identity to us.
4. The Son is the fulfillment of law and prophecy. How timeless of the Son not only to keep going after the degradation of the cross and the monumental triumph of the empty tomb but also never to waver one smidgen from his eternal purpose and promise. In completing the word of God down to the last ink spot, he has assured us his forever perseverance. Every word of Scripture is proof of his consuming love.
5. The Son came here to serve, to give, to die.
6. The Son seeks after and saves the lost.
7. The Son is the means of our salvation.
8. The Son rewards his people with eternal life.
9. The Son mediates between us and the Father.
10. The Son is the founder of the church.
11. The Son is the giver of true unity and peace.
12. The Son enables obedience in his disciples.
13. The Son demands our full trust and loyalty.
14. The Son is coming again.

Pray About

- Areas of doubt and worry that are clogging your faith walk.
- Cultivating a deeper desire to be captured by the Scriptures.
- What it means to be a follower of Christ, now and forever.

FIVE

GIFT OF A LIFETIME

I'm not surprised that when a chump left fielder with a so-so arm and a .275 batting average signs a multi-million-dollar, long-term contract, the watching sports world is amazed, stunned, and envious.

Nor am I surprised that when a billionaire blowhard finds another way to market his mystique, the tabloid buzz leaves the endless ranks of pop-culture connoisseurs amused, smiling, and entertained.

Jesus, however, when he came to Earth, wasn't going for either amazement or amusement. He wasn't looking to show off or to show anybody up.

He knew (as we sometimes forget) that comfort and control and name recognition can be difficult company. They're not satisfied with the sparse amenities in the spare bedroom or concerned that the rest of us have an early day tomorrow. They expect a little more. They expect to be treated differently. They expect to be fed, fawned over, and given to.

That's the trouble with takers. And the freedom of givers.

Lord Jesus, when we try to pour in anything but you, our boots leak, our cups run out. Teach us the secret of giving and of being thoroughly replenished.

The mother of Zebedee's sons approached [Jesus] with her sons. She knelt down to ask Him for something. "What do you want?" He asked her.

"Promise," she said to Him, "that these two sons of mine may sit, one on Your right and the other on Your left, in Your kingdom."

But Jesus answered, "You don't know what you're asking. Are you able to drink the cup that I am about to drink?"

"We are able," they said to Him.

He told them, "You will indeed drink My cup. *But to sit at My right and left is not Mine to give;* instead, it belongs to those for whom it has been prepared by My Father." When the 10 disciples heard this, they became indignant with the two brothers. But Jesus called them over and said, "You know that the rulers of the Gentiles dominate them, and the men of high position exercise power over them. *It must not be like that among you.* "On the contrary, whoever wants to become great among you must be your servant, and whoever wants to be first among you must be your slave; just as *the Son of Man did not come to be served, but to serve,* and to give His life—a ransom for many."

If the Bible were just a story, the foundation for a movie script, or a complex exercise in fictional character development, even then—*even then!*—you've got to figure the life of Jesus would be pure inspiration.

I mean, just watch him! When he could have pressured and pulled rank, he allowed his accusers to rant themselves into ignorance. When he could have sought to control and coerce his subjects, he chose to treat them instead as friends. When he could have rightfully made demands—even of God the Father himself—he willingly submitted to the plan that cost him his life, staying on mission no matter the cost.

His character is everything we really love in our truest big-screen heroes. The ability to show strong, deliberate mercy. The muscle to smother obvious, understood anger, replacing it with genuine love and sympathetic service. The grace to forgive, to restore hope and dignity to a human soul.

This is our Jesus. This is the Son of our universe. This is the one whose desire to save sinners kept him from saving even himself, placing a new summit and standard on obedience while demonstrating a heart for people that no living being has ever come close to, much less eclipsed.

READ
HEBREWS 5:5–10

HEAD DOWN, EYES OPEN

When Jesus looked into people's eyes, he wasn't sizing them up for acceptance. Unlike us, he wasn't immediately clicking through a Rolodex of value judgments—wondering how anyone's teeth could be so perfect or nose so unusual, trying to come within five years of her age by counting the smile lines or guessing her real hair color.

He taught us instead to look at people's feet.

Everyone has them. No matter how curvy the figure or how crisp the starched creases, no one wanders into our lives without feet, without unresolved issues, without unmet needs, and usually without wanting us to know about it.

Feet are our equalizers. Even the best looking of them can reveal some odd shapes and angular abnormalities, a functional design never meant to impress but simply to keep us from crawling on our hands and knees.

Yet we kid ourselves by thinking we can walk upright forever without needing anyone else's help, without exposing our hearts, without depending on another.

And we fail to be like Christ when we choose not to notice the feet of our friends, the feet of our family, the feet of those who need

READ
JOHN 13:12–17

the Jesus in us—the Jesus who's already washed our feet many more times than we'd like to admit.

Endless Love

Always remember, though—boy, and isn't this a jump-up-and-down reality of Christian living—that it's one thing to be motivated by and want to be like Mother Teresa, or the missionary who ministers to AIDS patients in Ethiopia, or the little girl on the home makeover show who cares more about the kids in her old cancer ward than about getting her own dolled-up dream house.

But in desiring to be like Christ, in letting his care and nourishment and supply and compassion pour out through our own open arms and hearts, the Bible tells us that something mystically marvelous happens. *We not only serve another person; we also serve the Son.* "I assure you: Whatever you did for one of the least of these brothers of Mine, you did for Me" (MATT. 25:40).

Usually the person who pays for dinner is amply satisfied just by being thanked. And yet Jesus, the sole provider of the love we share with others, gives us the bonus opportunity of ministering to *him* through our acts of service to *them*. When he reaches through us to bless our children, neighbors, coworkers, and friends, he fills us as well with the blessings of worship.

Truly, in all the years we've known him, the Son has never stopped giving us more than we asked for, more than we came for, more than we even knew we needed.

Oh, to be like him.

READ
JOHN 15:11–14

DIG IN

For all of us who've ever wanted dibs on Jesus' attention, Matthew 20 reminds us that it's not about what we want.

"To sit at My right and left is not Mine to give" (v. 24). How do we get ourselves so far afield from the heartbeat of God? Where do we come off thinking we outrank other believers?

....
....
....
....
....

"It must not be like that among you" (v. 26). *Must* and *must not* should be words that get our attention. How seriously are you taking this "must not" of Jesus?

....
....
....
....
....

"The Son of Man did not come to be served, but to serve" (v. 28). What keeps us glad that Jesus was like this but not inspired enough to want to be like him?

....
....
....
....
....

Experiencing God the Son Over and Over Again

1. The Son has the Father's blessing and approval.

2. The Son seeks and carries out the Father's will.

3. The Son reveals the Father's identity to us.

4. The Son is the fulfillment of law and prophecy.

5. The Son came here to serve, to give, to die.
   Great leaders must do more than string a few inspiring words together. They must also demonstrate that they believe their own words enough to live like they mean them. In Jesus we see someone with not only the courage to stand behind his words but also the willingness to kneel down to meet them. And the call on every disciple of Christ is to join him on our knees.

6. The Son seeks after and saves the lost.

7. The Son is the means of our salvation.

8. The Son rewards his people with eternal life.

9. The Son mediates between us and the Father.

10. The Son is the founder of the church.

11. The Son is the giver of true unity and peace.

12. The Son enables obedience in his disciples.

13. The Son demands our full trust and loyalty.

14. The Son is coming again.

Pray About

- Achieving a new reverence for the humility of Christ.
- Seeking the change of heart that will lead to greater service.
- The people in your world who need what Jesus can give.

SIX
LOST AND FOUND

We're number one.

I'm not talking about better-than-everybody-else number one. Or we're-the-champs-and-you're-not number one. Or na-na-na-na, hey-hey-hey, good-bye number one.

I'm talking about the Good Shepherd's number one. The missing-lamb number one. The one-hundred-minus-ninety-nine number one.

In him we can say it. Without risk of pride or self-gloating superiority. We're the "no one who believes on Him will be put to shame" number one. The "everyone who calls on the name of the Lord will be saved" number one. The "with the heart one believes" number one, "with the mouth one confesses" number one, "not the will of your Father that one of these little ones perish" number one.

Oh, one day we were less than number one. All-have-sinned number one. No-not-one number one. Then along came the Holy-and-Righteous One. The Faithful-and-True One. The Living One . . . who sought us, and loved us, and saved us, and made us his own number one.

Lord Jesus, you're a lifesaver. You've done something for me I was helpless to accomplish. Count me grateful.

[Jesus] entered Jericho and was passing through. There was a man named Zacchaeus who was a chief tax collector, and he was rich. He was trying to see who Jesus was, but he was not able because of the crowd, since he was a short man. So running ahead, he climbed up a sycamore tree to see Jesus, since He was about to pass that way. When Jesus came to the place, He looked up and said to him, "Zacchaeus, *hurry and come down, because today I must stay at your house.*"

So he quickly came down and welcomed Him joyfully. All who saw it began to complain, *"He's gone to lodge with a sinful man!"*

But Zacchaeus stood there and said to the Lord, "Look, I'll give half of my possessions to the poor, Lord! And if I have extorted anything from anyone, I'll pay back four times as much!"

"Today salvation has come to this house," Jesus told him, "because he too is a son of Abraham. *For the Son of Man has come to seek and to save the lost.*"

There may not be another story in all the Bible that brings out the kid in us like the story of Zacchaeus. Maybe it's the song. Maybe it's the sycamore tree. I don't know.

But what probably appeals to us the most is the picture we get of the jostling crowd, the shoulder-to-shoulder crush of bodies on a Middle Eastern street, the dust being scuffled up, the heat baking down, and Zacchaeus, leaping his little frame for a better look.

Of all the people for Jesus to notice. Of all the citizens of Jericho for the Son of God to take a shine to. But it really shouldn't surprise us that he singled Zacchaeus out. After all, six-foot, standard-issue, self-sufficient hearts aren't usually the ones who would want a whole day and dinner with Jesus anyway.

Yes, it seems like the Son was always turning his attention to people who already knew how short they were. Like the woman who for more than eighteen years had been bent nearly double by some strange abnormality. When Jesus saw her, clear across the crowded synagogue, "He called out to her, 'Woman, you are free of your disability'" (LUKE 13:12).

That's just who he was. Wisdom to the foolish. Strength for the weak. And the gift of renewed stature to those who had come to realize (like Zacchaeus), through lots of cheating and shell games and compromises with his character, that he was the last person on earth who could ever measure up to God's standards.

READ
1 CORINTHIANS
1:26–31

That's the kind of guy the Son of God came to stand tall for.

WORSE THAN IT

SEEMS

There's another low-down person who comes to mind when you think of Christ seeking and saving the least and the lost. Think of the woman who snuck into Simon the Pharisee's house, "an alabaster flask of fragrant oil" in her hands (LUKE 7:37). How surreal it must have seemed as the sudden smell of thick perfume began breaking off conversations in mid-sentence, the hum of the house slowly thinning into silence.

How did she get in here? Simon must have sneered to himself. "This man, if He were a prophet, would know who and what kind of woman this is who is touching Him" (v. 39).

Yes, Jesus knew who she was, all right—a woman whose slop bucket of sins had gotten much heavier than most, someone who had grown so accustomed to guilt's dead weight, she more quickly noticed the contrast when everything around her had become lightness and freedom in the face of Christ.

I used to read this story and feel almost cheated. How could I, a good Christian boy, raised on prayer meetings and after-church potlucks, ever hope to "love much" the way this woman did? Was I destined to be the one who, being "forgiven little," could never do more than "love little"? (v. 47).

What pious pride! Don't I realize that I, too, have been forgiven much, that we *all*—hopeless, heartless, hypocrites in hiding—were soiled in our own filth just like every drug dealer and two-timer Jesus found in their misery and saved from destruction?

READ
EPHESIANS 2:1–5

BROUGHT UP RIGHT

This is why the Son came here. Not to reward the already righteous. Not to pick teams from the obviously talented. He came seeking those who were short on self-esteem and low on available options, who had finally reached the point of being totally disillusioned and utterly dreamed out.

To some this seems like an extremely weak spot from which to launch a successful life. Not exactly the kind of attitude that makes you stand out for a promotion or paints a good case for a raise.

But ask Zacchaeus how high you can stand when you've been with Jesus, how much of a raise you can get by making things right with him and passing out the tax refunds.

It's short guys like him—and sinners like us—who know we could never have gotten pulled to our feet if Jesus hadn't come along when he did.

READ
GALATIANS 4:4–7

DIG IN

Sure enough, the story of the wee little man from Luke 19 has a lot to teach us about the larger-than-life Son of Man.

"HURRY AND COME DOWN, BECAUSE TODAY I MUST STAY AT YOUR HOUSE" (v. 5). What significance do you place on the fact that Jesus wanted to come into Zacchaeus's living space?

....
....
....
....
....

"HE'S GONE TO LODGE WITH A SINFUL MAN!" (v. 7). What makes us assign letter grades to certain sins, while passing off our own as mistakes, weaknesses, or justifiable attitudes?

....
....
....
....
....

"THE SON OF MAN HAS COME TO SEEK AND TO SAVE THE LOST" (v. 10). Why was it not enough for him merely to save us? Why is it equally important that he also sought us?

....
....
....
....
....

Experiencing God the Son Over and Over Again

1. The Son has the Father's blessing and approval.
2. The Son seeks and carries out the Father's will.
3. The Son reveals the Father's identity to us.
4. The Son is the fulfillment of law and prophecy.
5. The Son came here to serve, to give, to die.
6. The Son seeks after and saves the lost.

   The fourteen statements on this page relate to the Son's character and ministry. Given enough space, we could have easily listed *ten times* that number and still not have come close to doing him justice. Yet this one particular action on his part is perhaps the most precious of all. He came here looking for us. And saved us from a future worse than death.

7. The Son is the means of our salvation.
8. The Son rewards his people with eternal life.
9. The Son mediates between us and the Father.
10. The Son is the founder of the church.
11. The Son is the giver of true unity and peace.
12. The Son enables obedience in his disciples.
13. The Son demands our full trust and loyalty.
14. The Son is coming again.

Pray About

- How much your salvation cost, how much it means to you.
- Your daily receptiveness to his freely given grace and mercy.
- Those people Christ desires to seek and save through you.

SEVEN
THE COMPLETE PACKAGE

The salvation aspect of the Son's ministry is far too vast and vital to be squeezed into just one of these chapters. So while the focus last time was on the *seeking* part of Jesus' salvation equation, this one deals more with the actual transaction—the part that gives the pursuit its purpose.

After all, if Jesus was just the loving, kindhearted, second-mile servant some people believe him to be, he could've reached out to us all he wanted to, making speeches and preaching unity. But if at the cross he had backed away from the Father's plan—or if (as some would prefer) we take the bloodstains out of the picture—we're left with a kind man who quit on us, a misguided mystic who talked a big game but couldn't deliver the goods.

The story of the gospel would not simply be *incomplete* without the Son's death. It would be incomprehensible. Like a calendar with no sevens. Like a word search puzzle with no vowels. Like a bottomless mailbox built over a storm drain.

Or like a good-intentioned person trying to save the world when we know good and well we can't even save a snowflake.

Lord Jesus, thank you for going through with it, for not only coming down to find me but also for making sure I had a place to go.

Therefore, since we have been declared righteous by faith, *we have peace with God through our Lord Jesus Christ.* Also through Him, we have obtained access by faith into this grace in which we stand, and we rejoice in the hope of the glory of God. And not only that, but we also rejoice in our afflictions, because we know that affliction produces endurance, endurance produces proven character, and proven character produces hope. This hope does not disappoint, because *God's love has been poured out in our hearts* through the Holy Spirit who was given to us.

For while we were still helpless, at the appointed moment, Christ died for the ungodly. For rarely will someone die for a just person—though for a good person perhaps someone might even dare to die. But God proves His own love for us in that *while we were still sinners, Christ died for us!* Much more then, since we have now been declared righteous by His blood, we will be saved through Him from wrath. For if, while we were enemies, we were reconciled to God through the death of His Son, [then how] much more, having been reconciled, will we be saved by His life!

I don't have to tell you what Jesus did for us. You already know how he fulfilled the law, walked the road, carried the cross, and took the punishment. How he bowed his bloodied head while forgiving his cold-eyed killers. How he yielded back the breath of life while declaring his mission complete.

This was the price of admission. This was the way it must be. This was the culminating moment that permanently disemboweled our sins like bank statements down a paper shredder.

If not for this pivotal event in both chronological and spiritual history, dealing with human sin would forever be like trying to put shaving cream back into the can, like pinning leaves back on tree limbs. The stain of guilt was deep and baked in, and our hearts bore all the dead-weight heaviness to prove it.

For generations, the priests had been carving up bulls and goats, "ministering and offering time after time the same sacrifices, which can never take away sins. But this man, after offering one sacrifice for sins forever, sat down at the right hand of God" (HEB. 10:11–12).

He was done. It was over. It was finished.

And it was perfect. "For by one offering He has perfected forever those who are sanctified" (V. 14). The Son's flawless life—complete in its humanity, eternal in its divinity—ripped sin's talons out by the roots and infused God's righteousness into the renewed spirits of the redeemed.

That's why we should never be content just to have memorized the *plan* of salvation. We need to fall in love again with the *face* of our salvation.

> READ
> HEBREWS 10:1–10

MEMBERS OF THE BORED?

I've got to admit, this story sometimes doesn't slow me down from sinning up a storm. I too often get a lot more joy out of my wife's lasagna than I do my Lord's deliverance.

Why is this so normal? Why have I watched *It's a Wonderful Life* three times this year and read the crucifixion account maybe once? Why do I make it a point each week to meditate on the *New York Times* Sunday crossword and not on the sole reason why Sunday should have any meaning for me at all?

Please tell me you're not like that.

It's not because we just need to get more excited about him. It's not because there's more we need to know.

I think this problem primarily arises from having lives habitually too full of things and appointments, of papers to grade and recycling to gather up. It's the result of demanding multi-master capacity in hearts built for only one.

But surely the Son of God, who became our perfect source of righteousness, wouldn't have come this far to leave us floundering in our faithlessness. Surely the power behind his death can become the power behind our own desire to need for less and to love him more.

READ
1 JOHN 1:1–4

FORGIVEN AND FREE

Maybe this'll help. Did you realize that because of Jesus' death on the cross, we don't follow rules anymore—we just follow Jesus? "What the law could not do since it was limited by the flesh, God did. He condemned sin in the flesh by sending His own Son in flesh like ours under sin's domain, and as a sin offering, *in order that the law's requirement would be accomplished in us*" (ROM. 8:3–4).

We're free! No spiritual clocks to punch, no formulas to follow. Jesus' death did it all. When we received his forgiveness by faith, God stamped A-pluses on every one of our papers. He not only scratched out all the failing grades of the past, but he even assured us straight 4.0s into the future.

Therefore, we're like people living on the truly unlimited resources of a rich relative . . . with one big choice to make. Do we really want to abuse this privilege by making ourselves the center of

READ
1 THESSALONIANS
1:5–10

our universe, or will we let this newfound windfall become our freedom to break out in blessings, to pour our big Brother's love into other people's lives?

DIG IN

Paul's work in the book of Romans couldn't possibly be more full of both logic and life. Like in chapter 5.

"WE HAVE PEACE WITH GOD THROUGH OUR LORD JESUS CHRIST" (v. 1). This "peace" is more of a fact than a feeling. But still, has anything been keeping you from feeling it lately?

....

....

....

....

....

"GOD'S LOVE HAS BEEN POURED OUT IN OUR HEARTS" (v. 5). Again, this is not some squishy feeling. It's a cool, clear fact of our salvation. What do you make of God's love for you?

....

....

....

....

....

"WHILE WE WERE STILL SINNERS, CHRIST DIED FOR US" (v. 8). We don't have any way to know what it means to die for someone else. But what should we know about being died for?

....

....

....

....

....

Experiencing God the Son Over and Over Again

1. The Son has the Father's blessing and approval.
2. The Son seeks and carries out the Father's will.
3. The Son reveals the Father's identity to us.
4. The Son is the fulfillment of law and prophecy.
5. The Son came here to serve, to give, to die.
6. The Son seeks after and saves the lost.
7. The Son is the means of our salvation.

   The "substitutionary death" of Christ is hard for us to grasp. How does it work? Why does one man's death mean life for me? Honestly, it's simply the loving plan of the Father, who made "the One who did not know sin to be sin for us, so that we might become the righteousness of God in Him" (2 COR. 5:21). It keeps him perfectly just. It keeps us perfectly saved.

8. The Son rewards his people with eternal life.
9. The Son mediates between us and the Father.
10. The Son is the founder of the church.
11. The Son is the giver of true unity and peace.
12. The Son enables obedience in his disciples.
13. The Son demands our full trust and loyalty.
14. The Son is coming again.

Pray About

- The hunger to live as though this is all that really matters.
- The power to experience victory over the sins in your life.
- The willingness to share this news without fail, without fear.

EIGHT

COME INTO
THE LIFE

We all know people who've never gotten past a certain day. The day their heart was broken by an unfaithful spouse. The day their dream of achieving a lifelong goal was either shattered by their own failure or rendered hopeless through the shrinking of years.

Even *good* things have the potential to paralyze us. Some people, for example, continue to live in the afterglow of past glories and achievements, either too comfortable or too afraid to risk living in the present.

The problem with such stagnation, of course, is that life comes packaged fresh every day, not sold in bulk or held back for later delivery. Of course, not every day looks, feels, or smells the same. Not every day is one we really look forward to opening the drapes for. But each one is important. And each one begs to be lived . . . even if it requires more courage than we currently have in reserve.

That's why it's so essential that we don't relegate the cross of Christ to something that merely saves us from the past. Yes, his death has sufficiently dealt with yesterday's problems. But it also gives us new life for today. Even *this* day.

Lord Jesus, never let me grow ungrateful for how you released me of my sin load. But show me what it means to live without it.

Now if Christ is preached as raised from the dead, *how can some of you say, "There is no resurrection of the dead"?* But if there is no resurrection of the dead, then Christ has not been raised; and if Christ has not been raised, then our preaching is without foundation, and so is your faith. In addition, we are found to be false witnesses about God, because we have testified about God that He raised up Christ—whom He did not raise up if in fact the dead are not raised. For if the dead are not raised, Christ has not been raised. And *if Christ has not been raised, your faith is worthless;* you are still in your sins.

Therefore those who have fallen asleep in Christ have also perished. If we have placed our hope in Christ for this life only, we should be pitied more than anyone.

But now Christ has been raised from the dead, *the firstfruits of those who have fallen asleep.* For since death came through a man, the resurrection of the dead also comes through a man. For just as in Adam all die, so also in Christ all will be made alive.

If you take all the furniture out of the den, you'll probably feel really good about seeing that hand-me-down sofa on the back of the truck and on its way to the salvage store. But you won't have anyplace to sit and watch television later.

Empty everything out of the fridge and, though it's good to know that the brown lettuce and other unidentifiable leftovers have quit soaking up all the baking soda, you won't have anything to fix for supper tonight.

Obviously, it's not enough to just get rid of stuff unless you put something better in its place.

Jesus certainly knew this. That's pretty much what he was proposing one day while standing over the stretcher of a helpless paralytic.

"Which is easier?" he asked. "To say, 'Your sins are forgiven you,' or to say, 'Get up and walk'?" (LUKE 5:23)—*to say, "I've taken care of your past," or "I've stripped the limits off your future"*?

Nothing like a good question from Jesus to make as much sense now as it did two thousand years ago. Yes, Jesus' flesh and blood did indeed serve up the perfect sacrifice for our sin. Thanks to him, we're totally forgiven. But he also ensured that we could be much more than mere healed bodies, able to wiggle our toes and move our limbs, yet having nowhere worthwhile to take them.

Truly, when the Son set us free, he also turned us loose—not just to be nonslaves but to be real-live friends.

READ
JOHN 6:53–58

THE BEST, ONLY BETTER

This is both the beauty and the power of his death and of his resurrection. This is the side of the coin that transforms Christianity from being a drudge of one-dimensional sin avoidance into a daily experience of God's eternal riches.

As a spiritual writer of another day put it: "If a Christian limits God's redemptive work by being content with merely overcoming sin, he falls short of the purpose of God." Yes, Jesus' death did a lot more than trap and kill our iniquity. It sprung the door on life.

I mean, how else can you interpret a passage like this: "God has given us eternal life, and this life is in His Son. The one who has the Son has life. The one who doesn't have the Son of God does not have life. I have written these things to you who believe in the name of the Son of God, so that you may know that you have eternal life" (1 JOHN 5:11–13).

Good grief, if John had been any clearer, we could have seen his food digesting.

In fact, it was he who recorded these equally rich words of Christ earlier in his Gospel: "I am the door. If anyone enters by Me, he will be saved"—not merely to move out of the cellar but into the fresh air—to "come in and go out and find pasture" (John 10:9), to experience a freedom of movement unbridled by fear, unhindered by religious duty and do-gooding.

If we'll let it, this can be our description of life with Christ. In and out. There and back. Led by the one who left our past in a saving swirl of dust.

READ
ROMANS 6:8–11

GREAT DAY IN THE MORNING

I hope you don't hear me making light of tough situations that are understandably hard to overcome, sheer mountain climbs out of guilt and grief, out of disillusionment and depression. I also hope you don't hear me saying that forgiveness isn't something to savor and celebrate.

But the Son's mission is (and has always been) to release us from bondage and then send us into action, to clear the decks and then set us steaming for home. Just ask the woman who'd been "caught in the act of committing adultery" (JOHN 8:4). Ask her about the Jesus who could have stopped at letting her off but wouldn't quit until he'd pointed her on.

Sure, nothing good was going to happen in our lives until our sin had been dismantled. But now that it is, we're free to explore, expect, and experience all that God wants to do with us by this time tomorrow . . . another day in a life that's been secured by the Son.

READ
JOHN 3:13–17

DIG IN

You can't understand Christ's death without seeing it beside his resurrection. That's the compelling point of 1 Corinthians 15.

"How can some of you say, 'There is no resurrection of the dead'?" (v. 12). What makes so many in the church today unwilling to believe that the Bible means what it says?

....
....
....
....
....

"If Christ has not been raised, your faith is worthless" (v. 17). What would be the implications of a dead Jesus, a tomb still visited today by his devoted followers?

....
....
....
....
....

"The firstfruits of those who have fallen asleep" (v. 20). How has resurrection changed you? What difference does this forever promise bring to your life today?

....
....
....
....
....

Experiencing God the Son Over and Over Again

1. The Son has the Father's blessing and approval.
2. The Son seeks and carries out the Father's will.
3. The Son reveals the Father's identity to us.
4. The Son is the fulfillment of law and prophecy.
5. The Son came here to serve, to give, to die.
6. The Son seeks after and saves the lost.
7. The Son is the means of our salvation.
8. The Son rewards his people with eternal life.

   This is the third in a trinity of blessings that surround our salvation experience—the fact that he sought us, absolved us, and infused us with new life. One without the other is not enough. All are necessary to make us who we are. And all have been accomplished through the love and power of the Son of God. Indeed, "death has been swallowed up in victory" (1 Cor. 15:54).

9. The Son mediates between us and the Father.
10. The Son is the founder of the church.
11. The Son is the giver of true unity and peace.
12. The Son enables obedience in his disciples.
13. The Son demands our full trust and loyalty.
14. The Son is coming again.

Pray About

- Your own daily experience of resurrection freedom.
- Wounds from the past that need Christ's healing touch.
- Anything that's keeping you from moving in, moving on.

NINE

IN JESUS' NAME

As prepositions go, *between* is one of the longest there is. But why shouldn't it be?

I mean, if it weren't for *between*, we'd never enjoy that extra little bun in the middle of a Big Mac. Or the warm blanket that goes between us and the bedspread on a really cold night.

We'd never have a halftime show to strike up the marching band—the drums and bugles, the bells and whistles, the formations, the '50s hits, the flag girls.

There'd never be a middle child, or any letters except A and Z, no numbers to choose from between one and one hundred.

Hey, without *between,* we'd have never even gotten to see *Rocky II, III,* or *IV*—just the first one where he lost at the end, and the rotten fifth one that still owes me my five dollars back. (Of course, we'd also never be subjected to another straight-to-video preview of *The Land Before Time XIV* either. Some *betweens* we can live without.)

But not without Jesus, who stands between us and the Father, between now and forever.

Lord Jesus, thank you for building the bridge that connects us with eternal life. May we walk it every day in humility and trust.

Hebrews 2:8–11, 14–15, 17–18

We do not yet see everything subjected to [man]. *But we do see Jesus*—"made lower than the angels for a short time" so that by God's grace He might taste death for everyone—*crowned with glory and honor* because of the suffering of death.

For it was fitting, in bringing many sons to glory, that He, for whom and through whom all things exist, should make the source of their salvation perfect through sufferings. For the One who sanctifies and those who are sanctified all have one Father. That is why He is not ashamed to call them brothers. . . .

Now since the children have flesh and blood in common, He also shared in these, so that through His death He might destroy the one holding the power of death—that is, the Devil—and *free those who were held in slavery all their lives* by the fear of death. . . .

Therefore He had to be like His brothers in every way, so that He could become a merciful and faithful high priest in service to God, to make propitiation for the sins of the people. For *since* He Himself was tested and has suffered, *He is able to help those who are tested.*

Fortunately for us, we don't know what it's like not to have that "right hand of God" seat filled with its rightful, righteous occupant. A vacant chair would have meant empty hopes for every single one of us who've ever roamed the planet—down to the ones who give half their income to charity and rescue baby bunnies from the backyard.

That's because going to the Father without going through the Son is the most impossible task known to man—harder than scrubbing year-old juice stains out of the carpet, harder than busting rocks with a leaf rake, harder than getting somebody to answer the phone at the power company on a Saturday.

Impossible.

But because the Son is at God's right hand, because he's assumed his place of honor at the throne of grace, because he's fulfilled his role as "mediator of a new covenant" (Heb. 9:15), the light is on and the door's been left unlocked. We believers in Christ can now enter at will, being welcomed by the Son, ushered into glory, and received like family.

So if you're looking for proof that nothing is impossible with God, look no further than his right hand. See the Son. And experience a daily miracle.

> READ
> ROMANS 8:31–34

A LISTENING EAR

Theologically speaking, this great Bible doctrine of the high priesthood of Christ comes to us in the form of salvation. His once-for-all sacrifice of himself, the spotless Lamb of God, covers our sins and declares our slates cleaner than they were when they came from the factory.

But practically speaking, this truth comes to us at six in the morning when we're rousing from sleep, at three in the afternoon when we're in the car running errands, at ten at night when we clasp the hand of our sweetheart and rush together into the presence of God.

Prayer—that marvelous mystery that disguises itself as words floating harmlessly in air—is actually sweet communion between the Father and his children. And whether it glides on an invisible mist of silence, retraces its steps through routine requests, or paws its way across waves of emotion—of fear or dread or desperate need—prayer always rides on the back of the Son, from fingertip to fingertip, from us to the Father.

So "ask Me anything in My name," Jesus said, as daring as that (JOHN 14:14). Whenever we read this verse, we usually start hoisting up disclaimers before we even get the words out of our mouths.

But maybe our fear to ask for big things is as wrong as our desire to ask for selfish things. Jesus is there. Listening. Interceding. We dare not waste our words as if they only matter to us.

READ
1 JOHN 5:14–15

A STAND-UP GUY

Stephen, the first to be martyred for the Christian faith, received a remarkable revelation into this truth in the fleeting moments before he died. With the snarling venom of the crowd reaching a menacing, uncontrollable volume, he raised his eyes toward heaven and saw a stunning sight.

Nearly singing his declaration, Stephen was dragged outside the city walls, lest his blasphemous blood stain the streets of Jerusalem, where volleys of hand-sized, hate-based stones could transform their indignation into justifiable homicide.

What had he said that finally pushed these people over the edge?

We know from MARK 16:19 that when Jesus was taken up to heaven, the Bible says he "sat down at the right hand of God." And in just about every New Testament location where this similar scenario is repeated, the inspired writers of Scripture portray Jesus as being seated by the Father's side, at rest in his holy presence.

But in Stephen's prayerful vision, Christ's chair was momentarily empty. And the one who had died to give Stephen his fearlessness of death had risen to his full stature. "I see the heavens opened," Stephen proclaimed, "and the Son of Man *standing* at the right hand of God!" (ACTS 7:56).

READ
HEBREWS 6:17–19

And this same Jesus stands up for us in resurrection power today, giving our hearts a place to call home.

DIG IN

Just about every inch of Hebrews is taken up with this high priesthood of Christ. Chapter 2 is as good an example as any.

"BUT WE DO SEE JESUS . . . CROWNED WITH GLORY AND HONOR" (V. 9). Definitely, what we see today is not the whole picture. What would help you be able to see Jesus more clearly?

....

....

....

....

....

"FREE THOSE WHO WERE HELD IN SLAVERY ALL THEIR LIVES" (V. 15). What would your life be like—how would it be different—if you could really put the fear of death behind you?

....

....

....

....

....

"HE IS ABLE TO HELP THOSE WHO ARE TESTED" (V. 18). He's been there. He knows. What difference does that make in the particular testing you're enduring right now?

....

....

....

....

Experiencing God the Son Over and Over Again

1. The Son has the Father's blessing and approval.
2. The Son seeks and carries out the Father's will.
3. The Son reveals the Father's identity to us.
4. The Son is the fulfillment of law and prophecy.
5. The Son came here to serve, to give, to die.
6. The Son seeks after and saves the lost.
7. The Son is the means of our salvation.
8. The Son rewards his people with eternal life.
9. The Son mediates between us and the Father.

   "Let us lay aside every weight and the sin that so easily ensnares us, and run with endurance the race that lies before us, keeping our eyes on Jesus, the source and perfecter of our faith, who for the joy that lay before Him endured a cross and despised the shame, and has sat down at the right hand of God's throne" (Heb. 12:1–2). That's where you'll find him.

10. The Son is the founder of the church.
11. The Son is the giver of true unity and peace.
12. The Son enables obedience in his disciples.
13. The Son demands our full trust and loyalty.
14. The Son is coming again.

Pray About

- The faith to know that Jesus is really there at his side.
- How you can be used of God during your times of testing.
- Those you know who are needlessly walking without him.

TEN

LEADER OF
THE PACK

The pastor of my boyhood church always maintained a simple severe weather policy: if you could get there, he'd be there.

And my parents were the "get there" type.

So although Sunday morning snow-ins in my part of the growing-up world weren't all that common, I can still remember a handful of times when we woke up to winter on the day of worship . . . and vowed to make sure our preacher wasn't there by himself.

In a sanctuary that usually boasted six or seven hundred people, I'd sit on one bench with my family of five, dotted behind and beside by two or three other lone adults—a husband who had come alone, an empty-nest couple, just ten or twelve of us—still huddled in our coats and having church.

No organ. No bulletin. No fanfare. No choir. Just my mom's lovely alto voice, my dad's, uh . . . voice, and the reading of Scripture, the informal prayers, the semblance of a sermon.

Yet Jesus was there. He's always there. Not to catch the show but to shepherd his flock, however few they may be.

Lord Jesus, church isn't always easy. But neither was the price you paid to establish it. Help us remember that.

May you be strengthened with all power, according to His glorious might, for all endurance and patience, with joy giving thanks to the Father, who has enabled you to share in the saints' inheritance in the light. He has rescued us from the domain of darkness *and transferred us into the kingdom of the Son He loves,* in whom we have redemption, the forgiveness of sins.

He is the image of the invisible God, the firstborn over all creation; because by Him everything was created, in heaven and on earth, the visible and the invisible, whether thrones or dominions or rulers or authorities—all things have been created through Him and for Him. *He is before all things, and by Him all things hold together.* He is also the head of the body, the church; He is the beginning, the firstborn from the dead, *so that He might come to have first place in everything.* For God was pleased [to have] all His fullness dwell in Him, and through Him to reconcile everything to Himself by making peace through the blood of His cross—whether things on earth or things in heaven.

There is no way adequately to reflect what it means when we say Christ is the "head of the body, the church" (COL. 1:18). It's not like he's the president, or the boss, or the chairman of the board, or the chief administrator. Those terms are all way too incomplete, far too confining.

That's because, truth is, Christ is the head "over *every* ruler and authority" (COL. 2:10). There is no higher law, no court of appeals, no review panel who can curtail his power or question his right to leadership.

Jesus is not merely in control, my friends. The church is his. It is him.

This means, of course, that it's not *ours.* Or the deacon board's. Or the budget committee's. Or old man So-and-So's, who'll probably never stop complaining about what the sound system does to his hearing aid.

This doesn't mean, now, that there aren't legitimate practices and positions to be challenged or defended. It doesn't mean that our involvement in the church should be passive and without opinion. But more than likely, just about all of us who truly love the church and care about its health and condition feel way too much ownership of it. We almost involuntarily seek to personalize it to our tastes and ministry preferences.

But this church is not ours and never will be or should be. It is now and will always be *his*, the one who "loved the church and gave Himself for her" (EPH. 5:25).

I SURRENDER ALL

READ
EPHESIANS 1:20–23

That last line, you probably remember, comes from the often talked-about passage in Ephesians 5 where Paul says wives should submit to their husbands "in everything" (V. 24).

How positively primeval, some say. I'd bet there's probably no other imperative in all the Bible that's rankled more hen feathers than that one.

But in reality this attitude of submission is one that applies to all of us. In Christ's eternal order of things, he is in charge, and his people are dependent upon his will and direction.

Yes, the leftover rebellion in us fights this single-link chain of command. And sure enough, it would be a rolling-boil recipe for tyranny if not for the fact that we who submit to Christ are placing our feelings and futures into the hands of one who loves us and leads us to one blessing after another.

That's why the wife who submits herself to a husband who's constantly thinking of her, sensitive to her needs and protective of her heart, is a woman who knows firsthand the meaning of the words *trust* and *security.* That's why the husband who refuses either to dominate or neglect his wife but who submits his will to Christ and treasures the bride he once kissed at a candlelit altar, brings a trickle-down (nay, pour-down) experience of blessing into their home.

The demanding of rights—either in church or in marriage—can never really give us what we want. But submission to Christ will always give us what *he* wants, and what more could we ever want?

READ
GALATIANS 2:19–20

COMPREHENSIVE COVERAGE

If you want a full-blown picture of Jesus in love with his church—his people—spend some time in the first three chapters of Revelation. Again you'll see the inadequacy of adjectives to describe his power and appearance: "His eyes like a fiery flame, His feet like fine bronze fired in a furnace, and His voice like the sound of cascading waters" (1:14–15).

The churches, then—the seven stars, reflecting his radiance—are all poised in the palm of his right hand. Protected from peril. Cradled in security.

And in his dictated letters to the churches of Asia, Jesus' words reveal a level of love and involvement that touch us with their intimacy. "I know your works. . . . I know where you live. . . . I know your tribulation and poverty."

See your church in his hand. Picture your particular needs on his

READ
REVELATION
3:20–21

mind and in his heart. Submit yourself again to the one who bore you, and keeps you, and will never let you go.

DIG IN

The superlatives of Colossians 1 are so grand and glorious, all you can really do is just stand there and worship.

"AND TRANSFERRED US INTO THE KINGDOM OF THE SON HE LOVES" (V. 13). The "kingdom" is bigger than the church. But how could your church better exemplify God's kingdom?

....

....

....

....

....

"HE IS BEFORE ALL THINGS, AND BY HIM ALL THINGS HOLD TOGETHER" (V. 17). We see this glue at work in everyday ways. But when do you wonder whether he's got things under control?

....

....

....

....

....

"SO THAT HE MIGHT COME TO HAVE FIRST PLACE IN EVERY-THING" (V. 18). Let this be the rally cry of your life and your church. What can you do to help this happen?

....

....

....

....

Experiencing God the Son Over and Over Again

1. The Son has the Father's blessing and approval.
2. The Son seeks and carries out the Father's will.
3. The Son reveals the Father's identity to us.
4. The Son is the fulfillment of law and prophecy.
5. The Son came here to serve, to give, to die.
6. The Son seeks after and saves the lost.
7. The Son is the means of our salvation.
8. The Son rewards his people with eternal life.
9. The Son mediates between us and the Father.
10. The Son is the founder of the church.

    People have tried down through the centuries to claim the church as their own. They've co-opted its authority, manipulated its message, and deified their own positions in its service. But no church can long avoid being transformed to museum status without recognizing Christ's true, authentic place at its head. We are his body, and we live at his pleasure.

11. The Son is the giver of true unity and peace.
12. The Son enables obedience in his disciples.
13. The Son demands our full trust and loyalty.
14. The Son is coming again.

Pray About

- Your own church—its greatest needs, its true potential.
- The church worldwide and your place in its community.
- The requisite brokenness that precedes God's blessing.

ELEVEN

THE
PEACEMAKER

I'm in full agreement with the notion that the church doesn't need to run the state or the state run the church. These two realms possess enough differences in their overall goals and objectives; they can't really cohere across the board under one banner. Even for Christians who rightfully decry our loss of freedoms and the ridiculous lengths to which some people have gone to strike God from our national vocabulary, few want the church to be running the whole show.

But what even the most radical defenders of church-and-state separation must be willing to deal with is this: they can go ahead and make *Jesus* a word to be hushed up and squeamish about, but they can't put peace and humanistic harmony in its place.

I mean, it seems like some believe that if they could get people to quit being whacked out on religion and more into recycling, they could manufacture a society where everybody gets along and the trains run on time.

But true peace requires a basis, a rationale. And like it or not, the only one that works over time is relationship with Jesus Christ.

Lord Jesus, I've been missing your peace lately. Help me to find it again and to seek it only in you.

At that time you were without the Messiah, excluded from the citizenship of Israel, and foreigners to the covenants of the promise, *with no hope and without God in the world.* But now in Christ Jesus, you who were far away have been brought near by the blood of the Messiah. *For He is our peace, who made both groups one* and tore down the dividing wall of hostility.

In His flesh He did away with the law of the commandments in regulations, so that He might create in Himself one new man from the two, resulting in peace.

[He did this so] that He might reconcile both to God in one body through the cross and put the hostility to death by it.

When Christ came, He proclaimed the good news of peace to you who were far away and peace to those who were near. For through Him we both have access by one Spirit to the Father. So then you are no longer foreigners and strangers, but fellow citizens with the saints, and members of God's household, built on the foundation of the apostles and prophets, with Christ Jesus Himself as the cornerstone.

It's on Christmas cards, Christmas bags, Christmas paper, Christmas yard art. "Peace on earth." We all like the sound of that.

But look a little closer inside any Bible other than the King James Version (not that I'm knocking it; I still carry a KJV myself sometimes), and you'll find something interesting about Luke 2:14. Here's the way this familiar angels-and-shepherds verse is rendered today, using the best linguistic resources available: "Peace on earth to people He favors," "to men on whom his favor rests" (NIV), "men with whom He is pleased" (NASB).

Now sink that down into your theological tank, and see what conclusions you draw.

We know from the balance of Scripture, of course, that no one pleases God on his own. "All have turned away, together they have

become useless; . . . and the path of peace they have not known"
(ROM. 3:12, 17). The only ones who have received his "favor" are
those who have received his Son as Savior and Lord.

So while "peace on earth" makes a really nice slogan at the
United Nations—and while people of all shapes, stripes, and sizes
should do everything we can to promote fairness and friendship
in our dealings with others—"peace" remains the
sole property of the believing heart. It's the exclu-
sive gift of Jesus Christ.

R E A D
JOHN 14:27

PEACE FOR THE KEEPING

As we've mentioned earlier, peace is more fact than feeling. It
must have grounds for existing—a reason for being—before it can
become a reliable companion.

That's why when Jesus spoke to the woman who had anointed
his feet with oil, he first said to her, "Your faith has saved you,"
before he could truthfully say, "Go in peace" (LUKE 7:50).

That's why he reserved the words "Peace to you!" as the
first thing he would say to his disciples after his resurrection
(JOHN 20:19). First the victory, then the declaration.

That's why "peace" became the standard greeting between
fellow believers in the early church: "Grace to you and peace from
God our Father and the Lord Jesus Christ" (ROM. 1:7).

The prophet Jeremiah had railed for years against the corrupt,
hypocritical leaders of Israel, those who went around claiming,
"Peace, peace, when there is no peace" (JER. 6:14). But in the after-
math of Jesus' ascension, in the afterglow that resonated through
his first-century followers, there were daily embraces punctuated
by "peace, peace" where *everywhere* was peace. Jesus had come and
made peace a functional reality.

That's why the "peace of the Messiah" can still be called upon
as an inner indicator of God's will and purpose (COL. 3:15)—
not a mere gut feeling or a hopeful hunch, but the deep, abiding,

I-just-know-it assurance that's only available to those who are living in open honesty with their heavenly peacemaker.

READ
MATTHEW 11:28–30

YOU AND UNITY

But it keeps getting better. That's because not only has Jesus come to give us peace with God, peace in our hearts, peace right down to the stripes on our tennis shoes; he has also made peace possible between us and others.

Oh, dear. People: the ultimate test of a Christian testimony.

But this is how the church we talked about in the last chapter becomes a real outpost of the kingdom of heaven, when "we who are many" actually start behaving like "one body in Christ and individually members of one another" (ROM. 12:5).

Our own experience has proven that this doesn't happen on its own. Type As and Type Bs, leaders and followers, control freaks and doormats, blue jeans and black suits—these colorful characters God has tossed together like plaids and stripes into the fabric of his family don't just naturally congregate into single-minded societies. If there's to be any meshing of this mixed bag—this melting pot—it's only going to happen when our hearts are consumed with Jesus and his will.

"From Him the whole body, fitted and knit together . . . , promotes the growth of the body" (EPH. 4:16)

READ
JOHN 17:20–23

and makes something unbelievable happen: peace on earth.

DIG IN

The distance and division described in Ephesians 2 brings to mind our same need for Christ's unity today.

"WITH NO HOPE AND WITHOUT GOD IN THE WORLD" (V. 12). It's hard to imagine a sadder statement or state of affairs. In what ways do you see this assessment in action today?

....

....

....

....

....

"FOR HE IS OUR PEACE, WHO MADE BOTH GROUPS ONE" (V. 14). This speaks, of course, to the Jew and Gentile division. But who else have you seen Christ unite from across the aisle?

....

....

....

....

....

"WHEN CHRIST CAME, HE PROCLAIMED THE GOOD NEWS OF PEACE" (V. 17). What examples of peace can you relate from your own heart in sharing this good news with others?

....

....

....

....

....

EXPERIENCING GOD THE SON
OVER AND OVER AGAIN

1. THE SON HAS THE FATHER'S BLESSING AND APPROVAL.
2. THE SON SEEKS AND CARRIES OUT THE FATHER'S WILL.
3. THE SON REVEALS THE FATHER'S IDENTITY TO US.
4. THE SON IS THE FULFILLMENT OF LAW AND PROPHECY.
5. THE SON CAME HERE TO SERVE, TO GIVE, TO DIE.
6. THE SON SEEKS AFTER AND SAVES THE LOST.
7. THE SON IS THE MEANS OF OUR SALVATION.
8. THE SON REWARDS HIS PEOPLE WITH ETERNAL LIFE.
9. THE SON MEDIATES BETWEEN US AND THE FATHER.
10. THE SON IS THE FOUNDER OF THE CHURCH.
11. THE SON IS THE GIVER OF TRUE UNITY AND PEACE.
    If you're a believer who's not experiencing peace in your heart, you can. If you're in a church that's not exemplifying peace in your fellowship, you can. Whatever "dividing wall" exists between you and unity—both personally and relationally—has already been dealt with by Christ's death and his death-defying power. He is your peace. Never forget that.
12. THE SON ENABLES OBEDIENCE IN HIS DISCIPLES.
13. THE SON DEMANDS OUR FULL TRUST AND LOYALTY.
14. THE SON IS COMING AGAIN.

PRAY ABOUT

- Situations in your life that are challenging your peace.
- Christ's desire to exhibit his tangible peace through you.
- How to really trust Christ for unity in your church.

TWELVE

STRAIGHT FROM THE VINE

There's not one of us Christians who doesn't struggle with certain sins. And we've all made gallant efforts at trying to put a stop to them.

We've made better lists to put us in more control of our day. We've made better use of the remote to keep us from seeing things we shouldn't. We've made better food choices, better friendships, used better language, picked better ways of expressing ourselves.

And, frankly, none of it has worked all that well. For the most part all we've done is create sin-management systems whose most notable quality is their reliability for springing leaks. All our *better* intentions and *better* goal settings haven't made us much *better* in the long run.

Maybe "better" is not really an option for this infatuated flesh of ours.

So after years of gathering data, our research indicates that if a dependable method of obedience is to be found, it's not going to start with anything that starts with us. It's going to start in the only place that anything truly good has ever happened in our lives.

If the Son was strong enough to save us, surely he can make us act like it.

Lord Jesus, I don't do a very good job of living for you. What I need is for you to live through me.

When they observed the boldness of Peter and John and realized that they were uneducated and untrained men, *they were amazed and knew that they had been with Jesus.* And since they saw the man who had been healed standing with them, they had nothing to say in response. After they had ordered them to leave the Sanhedrin, they conferred among themselves, saying, "What should we do with these men? For *an obvious sign,* evident to all who live in Jerusalem, *has been done through them, and we cannot deny it!* But so this does not spread any further among the people, let's threaten them against speaking to anyone in this name again." So they called for them and ordered them not to preach or teach at all in the name of Jesus.

But Peter and John answered them, "Whether it's right in the sight of God for us to listen to you rather than to God, you decide; for *we are unable to stop speaking about what we have seen and heard."*

After threatening them further, they released them. They found no way to punish them, because the people were all giving glory to God over what had been done.

My preacher friend Wayne Barber has a really good handle on what it means to be transformed by Christ, to let the righteousness we received (not earned) at salvation be the same righteousness we receive (not try to manufacture) the rest of our lives.

Wayne says that our flesh—our natural person, the one we brought with us at birth—only has two real ways of dealing with laws, rules, and commands. We can either choose *rebellion* against them (defying their authority), or we can choose *religiosity* toward them (enjoying our superiority). Either we do bad things, or we do good things. And we think we know which one of these God would prefer.

But the problem is, God is not pleased with our "good things." This is most clearly expressed, of course, in the familiar "filthy rags" phrase from Isaiah 64:6 (KJV). The only thing that pleases God is perfection, purity, unvarnished virtue. And not one of us can get within a Stone Age throw of that.

So if we're to satisfy our Father, we're going to have to appeal to the righteousness of another—the righteousness of the Son—not just to consider ourselves redeemed but to continue to live the Christ life.

In other words, there's a big difference between doing good things and being obedient. Obedience is a lot more *submission* to Christ than *commitment* to Christ.

> READ
> COLOSSIANS 3:9—11

ROOTS AND ALL

The picture Jesus painted of our relationship with him was of branches on a tree, of leafy appendages sprouting from a vine.

Now, if you've ever tried keeping the honeysuckles from taking over the hawthorn bush in your backyard, or the ivy from growing up the side of your house, you know that the strength of a vine sprig is not found in its exterior tendrils, where it curls up its flexible fingers and grows berries and stuff. The flimsy part that pokes up into the air can be ripped out fairly easily.

The trick, of course, is to try tracing its path—down, over, and through—until you finally come to the little stump in the ground where all this network of offshoots is coming from. And in the Christian life, this taproot—the initial source, the ground floor of vine growing—is the Son himself. As he said to his early followers, "You can do nothing without Me" (JOHN 15:5).

OK. Contrast that "nothing" with the "everything" of Philippians 4:13—"I am able to do *all things* through Him who strengthens me." And if you believe the Bible to be what it claims to be, you have to believe these statements are neither exaggerations nor extremes. "Nothing" means not even one little thing. "All things" means . . . "all things."

READ
ROMANS 13:11–14

And "I am able" necessarily translates into "[Jesus] strengthens me."

JESUS IN YOU

So when the high council asked Peter and John, "By what power or in whose name have you done this?"—this incredible healing—it wasn't spiritual-sounding jargon for them to answer, "By the name of Jesus Christ the Nazarene" (ACTS 4:7, 10).

When Paul and Barnabas (and countless others) were said to have "risked their lives for the name of the Lord Jesus Christ" (ACTS 15:26), they meant that Jesus could give his own courage to any believer living under threat of death. Even you. Even me.

Before Jesus commanded his followers to "go . . . and make disciples of all nations," he first assured them that "all authority has been given to Me in heaven and on earth" (MATT. 28:18–19). *No, you can't do this, but I can do this through you.*

That's why when Jesus said that we should "produce much fruit and prove to be My disciples" (JOHN 15:8), he wasn't laying down a dare. His "prove" didn't mean "Prove it!" It meant that our obedience to him would be the evidence that he was the one growing the fruit.

Can't just *anybody* do good things, like serving stew at the homeless shelter and giving money for disaster relief? Of course. God has been kind enough to extend his common grace over all mankind, so that none of us are as bad as we could be. But obedience to his will can only be performed by someone who is truly righteous.

And that someone is alive and ready to do some fruit-bearing in you today.

READ
2 CORINTHIANS 12:9–10

DIG IN

There was a point where Peter and John quit trying to do it all themselves. Acts 4 tells us what happened then.

"THEY WERE AMAZED AND KNEW THAT THEY HAD BEEN WITH JESUS" (V. 13). What would inspire people to make this kind of claim about us today? What would they need to see?

....

....

....

....

....

"AN OBVIOUS SIGN . . . HAS BEEN DONE THROUGH THEM, AND WE CANNOT DENY IT" (V. 16). What keeps our lives from being undeniably Christian? What stands in the way?

....

....

....

....

....

"WE ARE UNABLE TO STOP SPEAKING ABOUT WHAT WE HAVE SEEN AND HEARD" (V. 20). What are the costs of this kind of freedom, and what would make us willing to pay them?

....

....

....

....

....

Experiencing God the Son Over and Over Again

1. The Son has the Father's blessing and approval.
2. The Son seeks and carries out the Father's will.
3. The Son reveals the Father's identity to us.
4. The Son is the fulfillment of law and prophecy.
5. The Son came here to serve, to give, to die.
6. The Son seeks after and saves the lost.
7. The Son is the means of our salvation.
8. The Son rewards his people with eternal life.
9. The Son mediates between us and the Father.
10. The Son is the founder of the church.
11. The Son is the giver of true unity and peace.
12. The Son enables obedience in his disciples.
    We can't let this stop at being theological theory. You and I need to back off from trying to run our own lives and give Jesus room to pour himself out through us. He said, "Whatever you ask in My name, I will do it so that the Father may be glorified in the Son" (John 14:13). I've got a feeling that letting him drive the ship is one of those whatevers.
13. The Son demands our full trust and loyalty.
14. The Son is coming again.

Pray About

- A renewed desire to live by his Word, not by feelings.
- The daily discipline of letting his will take preeminence.
- A readiness to repent of the past and let him have the rest.

THIRTEEN

TOUGH
AS NAILS

The Son is kind and compassionate. We saw that when he welcomed little children into his sphere of blessing, when he noticed the weariness of the hungry and hurting crowds, when he told the grieving widow, "Don't cry," before raising her dead son to life.

The Son is also merciful and enduring. We saw that when he told Peter (predenial) that he was praying for him to stand firm and bounce back. We saw it when he stood there stoically, quietly suffering while pious power grabbers strutted their stuff and their smug accusations.

That's what usually comes to mind when we think of Jesus. Humble. Gracious. Peaceful.

So that's why a statement like this is a little hard to figure out: "Don't assume that I came to bring peace on the earth. I did not come to bring peace, but a sword" (MATT. 10:34). Son against father. Daughter against mother. "A man's enemies will be the members of his household" (MATT. 10:36).

This is supposed to be the evidence of his legacy?

Where's the gentle Jesus when you need him?

Lord Jesus, you have been so tender toward me, your love so all-encompassing. What am I to make of your hard words?

From then on Jesus began to point out to His disciples that He must go to Jerusalem and suffer many things from the elders, chief priests, and scribes, be killed, and be raised the third day. Then Peter took Him aside and began to rebuke Him, "Oh no, Lord! This will never happen to You!"

But He turned and told Peter, "Get behind Me, Satan! You are an offense to Me because *you're not thinking about God's concerns, but man's.*"

Then Jesus said to His disciples, "If anyone wants to come with Me, he must deny himself, take up his cross, and follow Me. For *whoever wants to save his life will lose it,* but whoever loses his life because of Me will find it. What will it benefit a man if he gains the whole world yet loses his life? Or *what will a man give in exchange for his life?*

For the Son of Man is going to come with His angels in the glory of His Father, and then He will reward each according to what he has done. I assure you: There are some standing here who will not taste death until they see the Son of Man coming in His kingdom."

I had coaches in Little League and high school who were vicious to my adolescent eyes. Their gaze terrified me. Their hollering of my last name made my breath go suddenly shallow.

But I'll tell you what: whenever they said, "Good job," it made me stand taller.

I had teachers whose tests and daily quizzes defied a student's ability to schmooze or sneak anything similar to semi-understanding past them without being instantly exposed. Their hours were dreaded. Their classrooms were houses of prayer.

But an *A* scrawled in their handwriting meant you'd really learned something.

You know what I'm saying? When every careless mistake is greeted with an "Aw, that's OK; nobody's perfect" . . . when sloppy work is routinely given the pass . . . when less than our best is considered acceptable under the circumstances, we'll consistently tend to give it little more than a lick and a promise, fully expecting sub-par to be close enough.

READ
LUKE 9:57–62

Is that the Jesus you really want?

CROSS CURRENT

Give me a Jesus who's honest about what a Christian life is supposed to look and feel like, who's not afraid to warn us to "sit down and calculate the cost" (LUKE 14:28), to see if suffering and sacrifice square with our spiritual expectations.

Give me a Jesus radical enough to utter things like, "Every one of you who does not say good-bye to all his possessions cannot be My disciple" (LUKE 14:33), rather than a here-and-now Messiah who's obsessed and preoccupied with the kind of car I'm driving.

Give me a Jesus willing to avoid the popularity his love and power deserved yet unwilling to send his followers off into the future underestimating the fact that "if they persecuted Me, they will also persecute you" (JOHN 15:20). "In fact, a time is coming when anyone who kills you will think he is offering service to God" (JOHN 16:2).

That's some heavy stuff. Those are some big demands to expect of people. That's why we needed the self-denying, take-up-your-cross mentality of Matthew 16. And though it may not be what we always want to hear, we'd better be good and glad he said it.

He knew we needed to know.

He knew we'd eventually come to a place where we wanted our pews to be plush and our sermons in multimedia animation on the big screen. He knew we'd get to where saying "God bless you" to someone seemed equivalent to sharing the gospel with them. He knew we'd lose our hunger for fasting and the disciplines of abiding in his presence, what with 130 channels to choose from and *Wheel of Fortune* to waste time on.

So hanging over our spineless hopes that Christian faith can peacefully coexist with comfort and luxury and a stack of *People* magazines, Jesus left us the indelible mark of the cross. *Our* cross. The serious reminder that Christian living is not about sidelining in spirituality. It's about the Son being our meat and drink and daily occupation.

READ:
ACTS 5:40–42

MULTIPLICATION AND DIVISION

Yes, Jesus' words could attract hate and anger. They still do. A single, steely-eyed statement of his could send the Pharisees spinning around to find the nearest available rock pile—*anything* to make this madman shut up!

He could be offensive to some. He still is. Even we who have been bought with his blood can find ourselves turned off by those who take him too seriously (we think), who don't mesh well in a world where acceptance is prized more highly than obedience.

And, yes, families can still divide over their various views of belief in him—some more savagely than others. The name of Christ brought up at such Thanksgiving dinner tables can receive everything from pitied smiles to obvious disapproval, from nervous squirmings to outright rudeness.

The name of Jesus still demands the taking of sides. Half in or half out isn't really a position you can maintain for long without being mightily outmatched by what life can throw at you.

But those ready to jump in with both feet—at all costs—will find their cup continually full, their perspectives progressively his, and their lives increasingly significant.

READ
GALATIANS 1:3–5

We'll be glad in the end that we carried our cross.

DIG IN

Jesus' challenge to the fully surrendered life finds its most memorable expression in the words of Matthew 16.

"You're not thinking about God's concerns, but man's" (v. 23). It's fairly shocking how sharply he rebuked Peter just for trying to help. But what was amiss in Peter's bravado?

....

....

....

....

....

"Whoever wants to save his life will lose it" (v. 25). The prospect of death humbles and horrifies us. But what are the character flaws exposed when we obsess in fear over death?

....

....

....

....

....

"What will a man give in exchange for his life?" (v. 26). Everybody wants his life to count for something. What have you seen result from the lives of faithful saints of God?

....

....

....

....

....

Experiencing God the Son Over and Over Again

1. THE SON HAS THE FATHER'S BLESSING AND APPROVAL.
2. THE SON SEEKS AND CARRIES OUT THE FATHER'S WILL.
3. THE SON REVEALS THE FATHER'S IDENTITY TO US.
4. THE SON IS THE FULFILLMENT OF LAW AND PROPHECY.
5. THE SON CAME HERE TO SERVE, TO GIVE, TO DIE.
6. THE SON SEEKS AFTER AND SAVES THE LOST.
7. THE SON IS THE MEANS OF OUR SALVATION.
8. THE SON REWARDS HIS PEOPLE WITH ETERNAL LIFE.
9. THE SON MEDIATES BETWEEN US AND THE FATHER.
10. THE SON IS THE FOUNDER OF THE CHURCH.
11. THE SON IS THE GIVER OF TRUE UNITY AND PEACE.
12. THE SON ENABLES OBEDIENCE IN HIS DISCIPLES.
13. THE SON DEMANDS OUR FULL TRUST AND LOYALTY.

    Ours is not a generation that can stomach too much gravity without mixing in some lighthearted banter. We admire the person who can inject a joke into a tense situation to break up the heaviness. But we should be glad that Jesus knew when to be serious, that he was assured enough in his own identity and reputation to shoot straight and pull no punches.

14. THE SON IS COMING AGAIN.

PRAY ABOUT

- Any softness you've allowed to develop in your life.
- A hunger to pray for those who are struggling to obey.
- Your willingness to be unliked if Christ's call demands it.

FOURTEEN

ENCORE
APPEARANCE

Although our forty-nine-dollar DVD player from the discount shop is mostly just play and rewind, and although the 1950s classics that make up our family's usual viewing fare don't always feature the latest innovations, I understand that some of the movies they release today on those big two-disk sets come with a choice of alternate endings.

Wow. (Our grandmas, who used to go to the black-and-white Saturday show for a nickel, would probably prescribe for us a day of weeding the bean patch to counteract such obvious spoiled rottenness.)

In the drama of real life, however, there have always been alternate endings proposed and advanced. Like coming back as a caterpillar or a crepe myrtle. Like being reabsorbed into the cosmos or floating peacefully in perpetual soul sleep.

But we are a people created to love and long for happy endings. And among the hundreds of options and opinions that exist in people's minds, only one has the power to send us out into the open air feeling warm, secure, smiling, laughing, anticipating.

The Son is coming again.

Come quickly, Lord Jesus. And until you do, help us await your return—our invisible hope—with visible faith and desire.

Then I heard something like the voice of a vast multitude, like the sound of cascading waters, and like the rumbling of loud thunder, saying: "Hallelujah—because our Lord God, the Almighty, has begun to reign! Let us be glad, rejoice, and give Him glory, because *the marriage of the Lamb has come, and His wife has prepared herself.*"

Then I saw heaven opened, and there was a white horse! Its rider is called Faithful and True, and in righteousness He judges and makes war. His eyes were like a fiery flame, and on His head were many crowns. *He had a name written that no one knows except Himself.* He wore a robe stained with blood, and His name is called the Word of God. *The armies* that were in heaven *followed Him on white horses, wearing pure white linen.* From His mouth came a sharp sword, so that with it He might strike the nations. He will shepherd them with an iron scepter. He will also trample the winepress of the fierce anger of God, the Almighty. And on His robe and on His thigh He has a name written: King of kings and Lord of lords.

I for one am glad that when Jesus comes again, he's not going to show up the way he did the first time—slowly emerging from within society, leaving us thirty years or more to sit around weighing the evidence, trying to figure out whether or not it's really him.

I guess, deep down, I can sort of sympathize with the early doubters of his divinity. Yes, the prophets had left hints to herald his coming but not in a way that made connecting the dots a clear-cut exercise.

I mean, I know the Son revealed himself to those who had ears to hear. I know he didn't leave people's acceptance of him totally up to their own intellect. But looking merely through human eyes, I can see why Jesus was understandably hard to believe in.

When he comes a second time, however—again according to the Scriptures—at least people won't be pondering his claims around the pottery wheel the way they did thousands of years ago. No, this time the prophecies are pretty plain: "He is coming with the clouds, and every eye will see Him, including those who pierced Him. . . . This is certain" (REV. 1:7). "For as the lightning comes from the east and flashes as far as the west, so will be the coming of the Son of Man" (MATT. 24:27).

And we are living in the age when the Bible says this could happen at any time. Right in the middle of a golf game, a garage sale, or a grocery run, the sky could rain glory, and a world we've known only through faith could become solid gold ground under our feet.

> READ
> DANIEL 7:13–14

How about that?

COMING AND GOING

But even with all this surety and excitement surrounding Christ's coming, we still tend to roll our eyes at anyone who acts like it could happen as easily this afternoon as it could six hundred years from now.

Oh, there are times in life when his coming sounds attractive and we seek it with a vengeance. Like when our bills have consistently outrun our income for six months in a row, and the options for covering our financial tracks are starting to seriously dwindle down toward zero. Like when the rebellion of one of our kids has filled our home with more hysterics than happiness. Like when our boss is just not letting up on us no matter how hard we work or what kind of strides we make.

That's when we're most likely to seek his dramatic rescue, to appeal for immediate relief.

Far too often, though, we'd be just as glad if he put things off till we could see our grandchildren born, or our business opportunity reach fruition, or our bulbs come up in the spring. Sometimes our hunger to see his face simply becomes crowded out with 1:00 meetings, getting the dog to the vet, renewing our car tags, or downloading our digital images and printing them out for a scrapbook.

We forget. We quit watching. We lose our edge. We lapse into apathy.

But the biblical report that his "coming is near" (JAMES 5:8) should mean more to us than the outside chance that "near" might mean sometime this decade. The Son's appearing should be "near" in our thoughts at any given moment of the day.

READ
1 THESSALONIANS
4:13–18

NEARER, STILL NEARER

So if this particular hour is catching you at a time when you're less interested in his return than about what you're having for dinner tonight—if you're looking forward more to the coming of football season than the coming of Christ—try letting this repeated phrase from Scripture become your new point of perspective:

"The Lord's coming is near."

For if we really have any sympathies for those who couldn't discern him in the first century, this tells us a lot more about ourselves than about them. Here we sit with a complete Bible lying open on our lap, God's power and promises pulsating in our ears like the regular, rhythmic ticking of a bedside timepiece. The only thing withheld from us concerning the return of Christ is the calendar date, the exact coordinates of his countdown. Yet even we have a hard time believing.

Why is that?

READ
HEBREWS 10:19–25

DIG IN

As Revelation 19 declares, the arrival of the Son will spell the end for some and just the beginning for others.

"THE MARRIAGE OF THE LAMB HAS COME, AND HIS WIFE HAS PREPARED HERSELF" (V. 7). There is only one way to prepare for this great and glorious day. Celebrate it in your own words:

....

....

....

....

"HE HAD A NAME WRITTEN THAT NO ONE KNOWS EXCEPT HIMSELF" (V. 12). Imagine a name too awesome to compress into words. Imagine the experience of seeing him in the clouds:

....

....

....

....

....

"THE ARMIES . . . FOLLOWED HIM ON WHITE HORSES, WEARING PURE WHITE LINEN" (V. 14). What would a whole day clothed in the pure white of Christ's righteousness look like to you?

....

....

....

....

....

Experiencing God the Son Over and Over Again

1. The Son has the Father's blessing and approval.
2. The Son seeks and carries out the Father's will.
3. The Son reveals the Father's identity to us.
4. The Son is the fulfillment of law and prophecy.
5. The Son came here to serve, to give, to die.
6. The Son seeks after and saves the lost.
7. The Son is the means of our salvation.
8. The Son rewards his people with eternal life.
9. The Son mediates between us and the Father.
10. The Son is the founder of the church.
11. The Son is the giver of true unity and peace.
12. The Son enables obedience in his disciples.
13. The Son demands our full trust and loyalty.
14. The Son is coming again.

   "Our citizenship is in heaven, from which we also eagerly wait for a Savior, the Lord Jesus Christ. He will transform the body of our humble condition into the likeness of His glorious body, by the power that enables Him to subject everything to Himself" (Phil. 3:20–21). And so we raise our united cry, "Maranatha!" (1 Cor. 16:22). *Our Lord come!* Whenever you're ready!

Pray About

- Your readiness and desire for life in his eternal kingdom.
- Those who continue to live under the curse of sin and death.
- The courage to place Christ at the forefront of everything.

ALSO AVAILABLE:
If you enjoyed using this book, try others in the series.

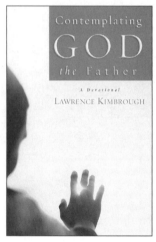

Contemplating God the Father
ISBN: 0-8054-4083-6

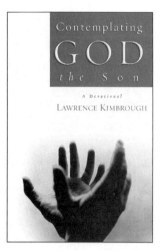

Contemplating God the Son
ISBN: 0-8054-4084-4

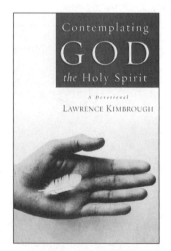

Contemplating God the Holy Spirit
ISBN: 0-8054-4085-2

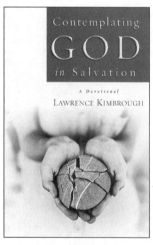

Contemplating God in Salvation
ISBN: 0-8054-4086-0

Find them in stores or at www.broadmanholman.com